NEWSMAKERS

IVANKA TRUMP

BUSINESSWOMAN AND POLITICAL ACTIVIST

BY BONNIE HINMAN

CONTENT CONSULTANT
Diana Hechavarría, Assistant Professor of Entrepreneurship
College of Business
University of South Florida

Cover image: Ivanka Trump speaks at the Republican National Convention.

Core Library
An Imprint of Abdo Publishing
abdopublishing.com

abdopublishing.com

Printed in the United States of America, North Mankato, Minnesota
022017
092017

THIS BOOK CONTAINS RECYCLED MATERIALS

Cover Photo: J. Scott Applewhite/AP Images
Interior Photos: J. Scott Applewhite/AP Images, 1, 10 (top left); Mark J. Terrill/AP Images, 4–5; Behar Anthony/SIPA USA/AP Images, 7; Evan Vucci/AP Images, 9, 38, 45; Zach Gibson/AP Images, 10 (top right), 10 (bottom left), 10 (bottom right); Ron Galella, Ltd./WireImage/Ron Galella Collection/Getty Images, 12–13; Shutterstock Images, 14, 20–21; Ron Galella/WireImage/Ron Galella Collection/Getty Images, 16; Mitchell Gerber/Corbis Entertainment/Getty Images, 18; iStockphoto, 23; Kittipong Kongwatmai/Shutterstock Images, 24; Charles Rex Arbogast/AP Images, 26–27; Mathew Imaging/Film Magic/Getty Images, 28; Bryan Steffy/Getty Images Entertainment/Getty Images, 30–31; Raoul Gatchalian/Star Max/AP Images, 34–35; Evan Agostini/AP Images, 36; Scott Olson/Getty Images News/Getty Images, 40

Editor: Alyssa Krekelberg
Imprint Designer: Maggie Villaume
Series Design Direction: Ryan Gale

Publisher's Cataloging-in-Publication Data

Names: Hinman, Bonnie, author.
Title: Ivanka Trump : businesswoman and political activist / by Bonnie Hinman.
Other titles: Businesswoman and political activist
Description: Minneapolis, MN : Abdo Publishing, 2018. | Series: Newsmakers | Includes bibliographical references and index.
Identifiers: LCCN 2016962127 | ISBN 9781532111860 (lib. bdg.) | ISBN 9781680789713 (ebook)
Subjects: LCSH: Trump, Ivanka, 1981- --Juvenile literature. | Businesspeople--United States--Biography--Juvenile literature. | Businesswomen--United States--Biography--Juvenile literature. | Women executives--Biography--Juvenile literature.
Classification: DDC 338 [B]--dc23
LC record available at http://lccn.loc.gov/2016962127

CONTENTS

CHAPTER ONE

STEALING THE SHOW

The Beatles song "Here Comes the Sun" boomed through the auditorium as Ivanka Trump walked onto the stage. Trump came to introduce her father, Donald Trump, at the Republican National Convention in Cleveland, Ohio. It was July 21, 2016, the last day of the four-day event. At the gathering, Republican leaders nominated Donald Trump as their candidate in the presidential election. Months later, Donald, a billionaire businessman and reality show star, would be elected the 45th president of the United States.

Ivanka Trump introduced her father, Donald Trump, at the Republican National Convention.

WHAT IS A POLITICAL CONVENTION?

American national political conventions were first held in 1831. Now, there are two major conventions each presidential election year. One is for the Republican Party. The other is for the Democratic Party. Members from each party meet in convention centers. They listen to speeches. Then they vote for the person they want to run for their party in the general election. The winner of the general election becomes president.

Donald picked his oldest daughter to introduce him to the delegates. It was not the first time Trump introduced her father to an audience. On June 16, 2015, she had introduced him at Trump Tower in New York City, New York. On that day, Donald had announced he was running for president.

MILLIONS WATCHING

At the convention, things were different for Trump. The audience for her speech included thousands of delegates, many reporters, and millions of viewers at home. The stakes were high.

During the last night of the Republican National Convention, Ivanka Trump praised her father.

The 34-year-old said in an interview that she was terrified to give the speech. She also said her father would not tell her what to say. He told his daughter not to worry. He said she would do a fine job.

He was right. Trump did not look terrified as she talked about her father. She spoke about her childhood and how her father supported her interest in business. She tried to soften the idea that her father was reckless. Donald spoke his mind, his daughter said, but he was a fighter and he got things done.

PARTY TIME

Many Americans are members of the Democratic or Republican parties. Other citizens call themselves Independents. They do not belong to any political party. A small number of citizens belong to minor political parties, such as the Green Party or the Libertarian Party. Throughout the United States' history there have been many other political parties. However, most of these parties did not last very long.

PRAISE FROM THE PUBLIC

People loved Trump's introduction. By the next day, even media members who did not like her father praised her. *Time* magazine said she was polite and

Donald Trump hugged his daughter, Ivanka Trump, after her speech.

MAJOR SPEAKERS AT THE 2016 REPUBLICAN NATIONAL CONVENTION

Monday, July 18

Melania Trump

Willie Robertson: Star of *Duck Dynasty* TV show
John Tiegen: US Marine Corps veteran; served in Benghazi, Libya
Melania Trump: Wife of Donald Trump

Tuesday, July 19

Ben Carson

Asa Hutchinson: Governor of Arkansas
Donald Trump Jr.: Son of Donald Trump
Ben Carson: Retired neurosurgeon and former Republican presidential candidate

Wednesday, July 20

Mike Pence

Michelle Van Etten: Small business owner
Darrell Scott: Pastor
Mike Pence: Governor of Indiana and vice presidential candidate

Thursday, July 21

Donald Trump

Peter Thiel: Entrepreneur
Ivanka Trump: Daughter of Donald Trump
Donald Trump: Presidential candidate

Speakers at the 2016 Republican National Convention came from many different backgrounds and jobs. Why do you think the Republican Party chose these speakers? How could these speakers argue in favor of Donald Trump and the Republican Party?

knowledgeable. Trump stole the show from her father and other speakers.

Trump's speech grabbed the public's attention. However, it was not the first time that people had noticed Trump. She was raised in the public eye by her rich parents. She had often been seen and talked about. Trump said her childhood was unusual but happy.

EXPLORE ONLINE

Chapter One talks about Ivanka Trump's speech at the 2016 Republican National Convention. The link below has more information on her speech. Compare and contrast this article and video clip to the information presented in Chapter One.

IVANKA TRUMP INTRODUCES HER FATHER

abdocorelibrary.com/ivanka-trump

CHAPTER TWO

GROWING UP RICH

Ivanka Trump was born on October 30, 1981, in New York City. Ivanka was the second child of Ivana and Donald Trump. She has an older brother, Donald Jr., and a younger brother, Eric. She also has a half-sister, Tiffany, and a half-brother, Barron.

Ivanka's mother, Ivana, was born in Czechoslovakia. After a career as a skier, Ivana became a model and moved to Canada. Eventually she ended up in New York City, where she met and married Donald Trump. Donald was born in Queens, New York. His grandparents came from Germany. Donald's father, Fred, started the family's construction

Eric, Ivanka, and Ivana Trump in 1993

Ivana Trump renovated the Plaza Hotel, *right*.

business. Donald later took over the business and turned it into a billion-dollar empire.

Ivanka's family lived in a large apartment in New York City's Trump Tower. Both of her parents worked long hours when Ivanka and her brothers were young. The older Trump children had nannies, and their grandparents were around much of the time.

PLAYTIME AT THE PLAZA

Ivanka remembers how much fun it was to follow her mother around as Ivana worked. Ivana supervised the renovation of the famous Plaza Hotel in New York City after Donald bought it in 1988. When the work was finished, Ivana managed the property. Ivanka first learned the importance of details from her mother.

Ivanka attended an elite girls' school

THE PLAZA HOTEL

The Plaza Hotel opened on October 1, 1907. The Plaza was in New York City's most fashionable area. Newspapers described it as the greatest hotel in the world. The designers spared no cost to make it look beautiful.

Donald Trump bought the hotel in 1988. Under Ivana Trump's supervision, the Plaza got new paint, furniture, and renovations. During this time the employees at the Plaza sometimes called Ivanka "Eloise." Eloise was the main character in a series of children's books published in 1955. The books were about a troublemaking little girl who lived on the top floor of the Plaza.

Ivana and Ivanka Trump in 1994

in New York City called Chapin. She and her brothers traveled with their parents. She says they had many luxuries but were taught that their parents worked hard. Ivanka, Eric, and Donald Jr. had been born into riches. However, they would have to work hard themselves to succeed in school and life.

TRUMP'S TEEN YEARS

Behind closed doors, Donald and Ivana were having marriage troubles. When Ivanka was nine years old, these problems became public. Months of newspaper stories followed. Her parents divorced in 1992. It was a hard time for the family. Ivanka said she became closer to her father during this time.

In 1996, Ivanka went away to Choate Rosemary Hall Boarding School for high school. On summer breaks, Ivanka and her brothers had jobs. They worked at different Trump properties. Ivanka also started modeling during high school.

Ivanka did not plan to become a model. Modeling agents had approached her when she was ten years old. She said no. When she was almost 15, an agent approached her again. By then she was interested in

FASHION MODEL

Fashion was a big business in the mid-1990s. There was a huge demand for models. Ivanka said her fellow models were mean. At that time many models were very thin. Trump was naturally tall and thin, but she had full cheeks. She called herself a baby-faced model. Fashion designers liked this look, too, even though it was not the typical look.

When she was 17 years old, Ivanka Trump modeled at the Marc Bouwer Fall Fashion Show.

fashion. She also realized she could earn her own money by modeling. She began working, but Ivanka also had educational goals in mind.

STRAIGHT TO THE SOURCE

In Trump's 2009 book, *The Trump Card: Playing to Win in Work and Life*, she wrote about how her parents taught their children good values:

> *My parents might have placed a special emphasis on our education and travel, but neither aspect of my childhood would have made much of a dent without the emphasis they also placed on hard work and dedication. No matter what we were doing, we were meant to do it to the best of our ability. And to pitch in. My brothers and I never really had a set list of chores we were meant to complete. Our household was too busy, too crazy for any kind of predictable routine. But if one of us was ever asked to do the dishes after dinner or put away the laundry, we were expected to do it right away, no questions asked. My parents had both been raised to follow orders, and they expected us to do so as well.*
>
> Source: Ivanka Trump. *The Trump Card: Playing to Win in Work and Life*. New York: Simon & Schuster, 2009. Print. 67.

Point of View

As the child of a billionaire, Ivanka could have decided to avoid hard work. Instead, she took on high school jobs. How might this experience have been useful to her?

CHAPTER THREE

COLLEGE AND THE WORKING WORLD

Trump started college at Georgetown University in Washington, DC, in 1999. After two years, she transferred to the Wharton School at the University of Pennsylvania. The school focused on business. During college, Trump realized she wanted to be a real estate developer like her father. She knew Donald would give her a job. However, she worried she would not be good enough to work in the family business.

One of Trump's professors at Wharton, Peter Linneman, suggested she work at

Ivanka, her brother Donald Jr., and her father all attended the Wharton School.

another business for a year or two. This would give her experience before she went to work for the Trump Organization.

THE TRUMP ORGANIZATION

Today, the Trump Organization handles businesses such as hotels, golf courses, and clothing lines. Donald Trump worked for his father, Fred Trump, after he graduated from college in 1968. In 1971 Donald took control of his father's company. In 1980 Donald named the company the Trump Organization. This company handled real estate projects in New York City. After years of success in real estate, the Trump Organization expanded into entertainment and merchandise. Today the Trump Organization employs more than 22,000 people.

STARTING A CAREER

With Linneman's advice in mind, Trump took a job with Forest City Ratner after graduating in 2004. This New York City company focused on real estate. Ratner was a family business much like the Trump Organization. Trump told them she would probably leave after a year or two.

Ivanka Trump learned how to make blueprints for buildings.

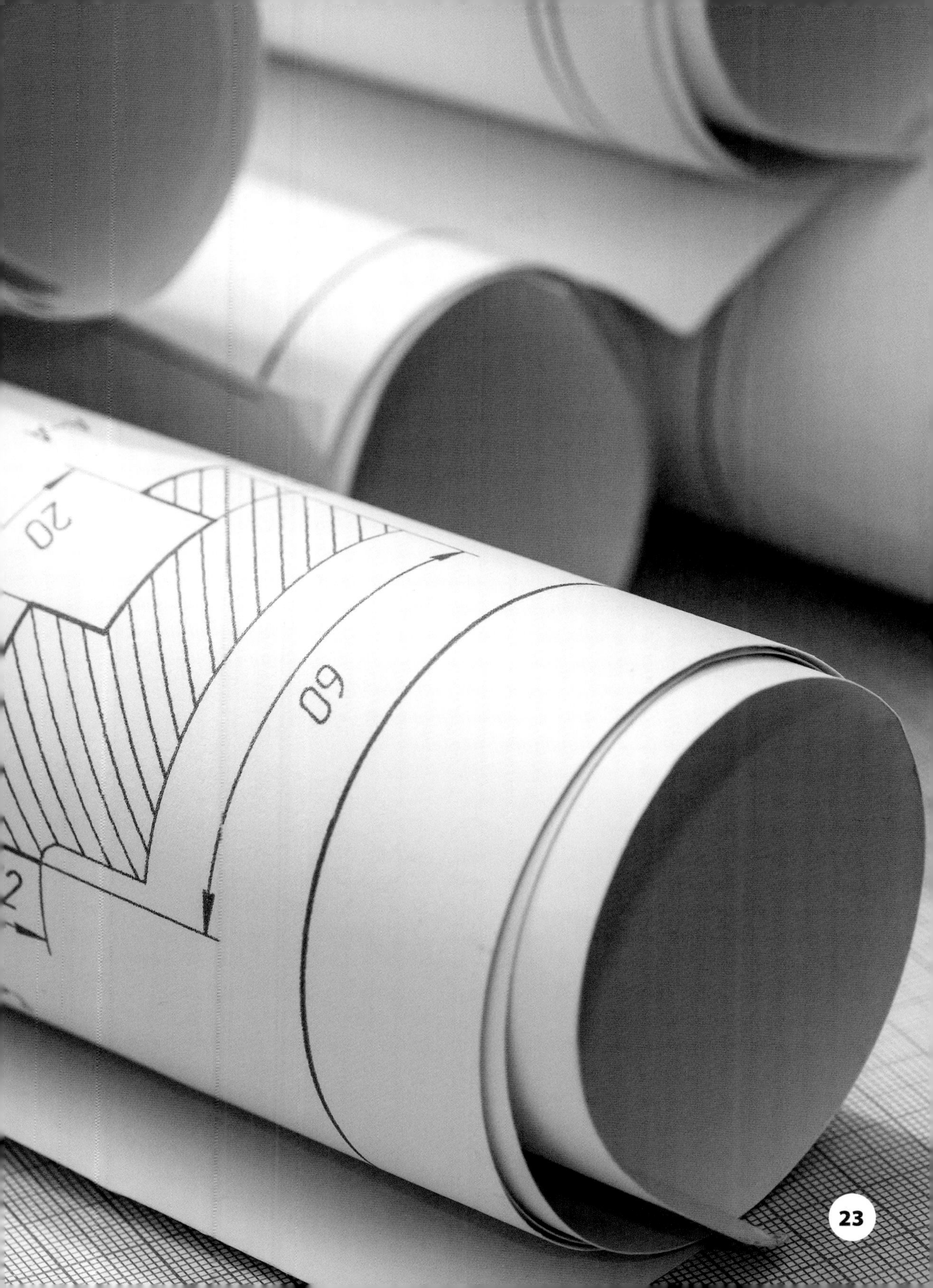

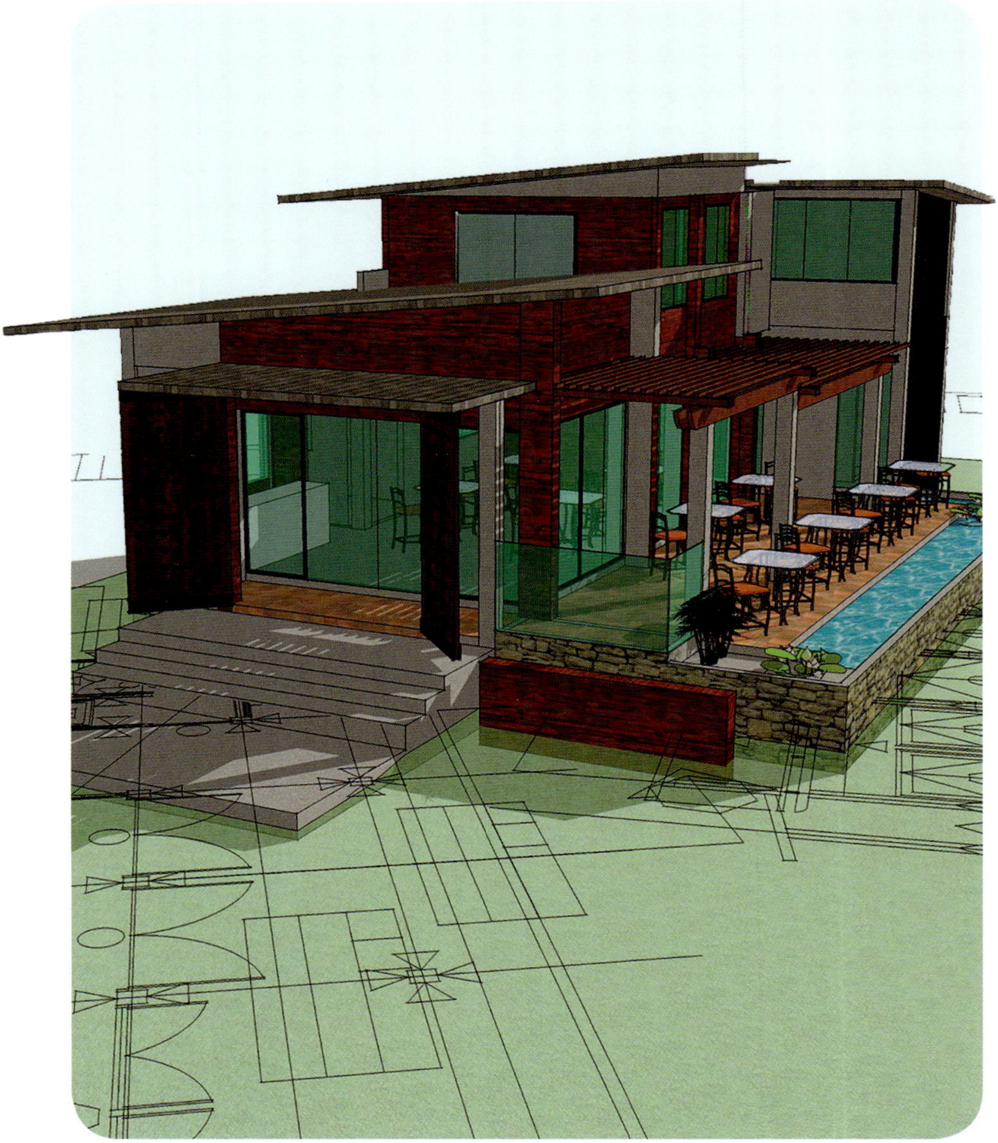

The computer program AutoCAD is used to create 3-D designs for buildings.

During Trump's time at Ratner, she helped develop a shopping center. Trump admits she did not have many skills to provide to the project at first. However, she attended meetings and planning sessions to learn all she could.

Trump also learned how to use AutoCAD in her free time at work. This is a computer program. It helps architects design blueprints for structures. Her bosses noticed her efforts to learn. When she quit after a year, they tried to get her to stay at Ratner.

Trump gained useful experience at Ratner. She felt confident about her skills. She was ready to work for the Trump Organization.

FURTHER EVIDENCE

Chapter Three focuses on Trump's experience in the working world. It shows how Trump handled her first full-time job at Forest City Ratner. The article at the following website offers advice for success at a person's first job. Did Trump use any of this advice at her first job?

6 TIPS TO ROCK YOUR FIRST JOB

abdocorelibrary.com/ivanka-trump

CHAPTER FOUR

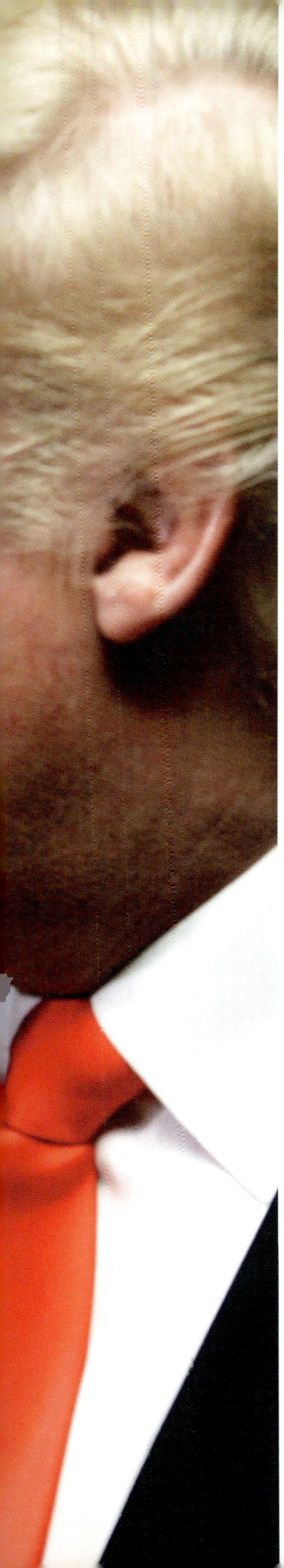

WORKING IN THE FAMILY BUSINESS

Trump started work at the Trump Organization in 2005. Her title was vice president of development and acquisitions. Her older brother, Donald Jr., had gone to work for their father in 2001. Her younger brother, Eric, would join the company in 2006.

Trump said she felt weighed down by her own expectations. She wanted to prove she deserved her job. She said she made mistakes.

Ivanka Trump joined her father's company in 2005.

She was nervous about asking for help. Eventually she learned asking for help was okay.

BUILDING A CAREER

Beginning in 2006, Trump started appearing on her father's television shows *The Apprentice* and *The Celebrity Apprentice*. These were reality shows. Contestants competed against each other. They were assigned different management, sales, or building projects. Trump would give her father advice before he fired a contestant each week.

TRUMP TELEVISION SHOWS

The television show *The Apprentice* brought 16 people to New York City and gave them tasks. Contestants had a mix of college degrees and street smarts. Two teams competed each week to see which one could complete their job assignments. Their success was judged by Donald Trump and his advisers. Ivanka Trump was one of the advisers from 2006 to 2015.

Ivanka Trump played a role in her father's television shows.

Pieces from Ivanka Trump's line of jewelry

In 2007 Trump and her brothers began Trump Hotels. Trump Hotels is a hotel management company. Hotels are often run by management companies. Trump Hotels supervised several hotels in the United States and other countries.

Trump also looked for properties on sale at a low price. If the owners could no longer afford a property,

they might sell it to the Trump Organization. Trump said they bought two golf courses this way.

TAKING A RISK

Trump took her first big personal business risk in 2007. She started Ivanka Trump Fine Jewelry. At that time, businesses wanted men to buy jewelry for women.

TRUMP ORGANIZATION
PROJECTS

Trump has worked on projects across the world for the Trump Organization. What do you think the challenges would be when working with so many distant locations?

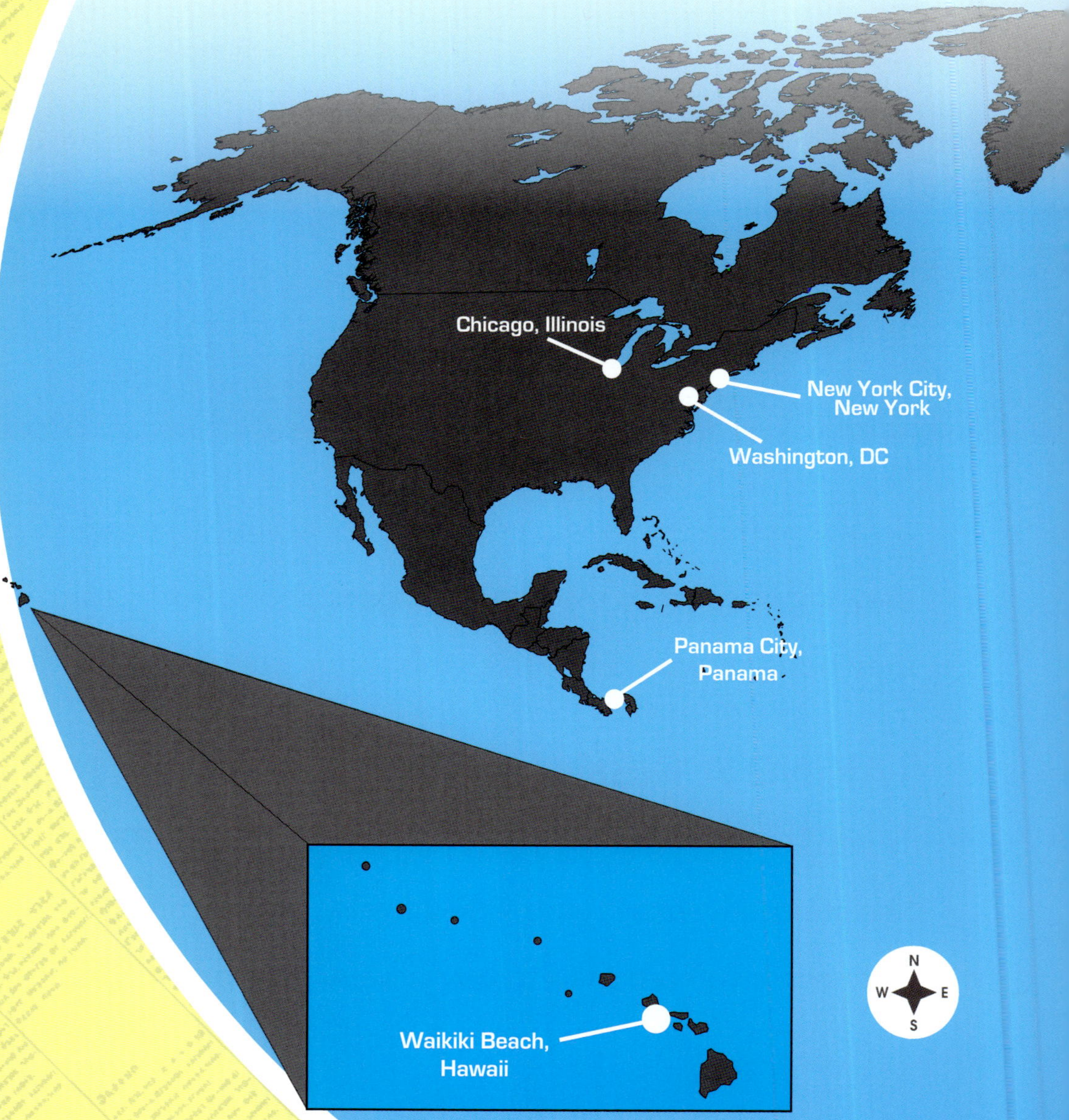

Trump wanted to create a company that targeted women buying jewelry for themselves.

Ivanka Trump Fine Jewelry has no connection to the Trump Organization. Trump's company continued to grow in spite of the economic recession that began in 2008. Trump's jewelry business sells rings, earrings, necklaces, and more.

RECESSION HITS THE UNITED STATES

Many developers went out of business during the United States' recession in 2008. They could not get money to construct buildings. Trump says the Trump Organization survived because it was doing hotel management. It did not build or own the hotels it managed. The company got through the hard times.

CHAPTER FIVE

PLAYING TO WIN

Trump received many calls for advice after she began appearing on *The Apprentice*. Women asked questions about how to become successful in business. Trump decided the best way to answer these questions was to write a book. In 2009, she published *The Trump Card: Playing to Win in Work and Life.*

That same year, Trump married Jared Kushner. Before her marriage, Trump converted to Kushner's religion, Judaism. She and Jared celebrate Jewish holidays. They also observe the Shabbat, which is a Jewish weekly family practice.

Trump appeared at a book signing in 2009.

NEW BUSINESS PROJECTS

After starting a jewelry business, Trump created a fashion company. It was called the Ivanka Trump Collection. This company sells items such as clothes and accessories. The popular department store chain Nordstrom sold Trump's products. However, Trump's fashion line has experienced some difficulties. After her father became president in 2017, Trump's fashion line began to suffer. Not as many people were buying her products. Nordstrom decided to stop selling items from the Ivanka Trump Collection.

WHAT IS SHABBAT?

Judaism is a religion. The Shabbat is a day of rest for Jews. Shabbat begins at sundown on Friday evening and lasts until Saturday evening. In Trump's family, this day of rest means they spend time together. Trump learned to cook so she could make a traditional Shabbat meal each Friday night.

Jared Kushner and Ivanka Trump married in 2009.

Ivanka Trump and Donald Trump attended the groundbreaking ceremony for the Trump International Hotel.

In addition to running her own companies, Trump continues to work for the Trump Organization. Trump was in charge of the $200 million renovation of the Old Post Office. This historic building is in Washington, DC. It was transformed into the Trump International Hotel. The new hotel opened in September 2016.

FAMILY DAYS

Trump and her husband have three children. Arabella, Joseph, and Theodore live with their parents in a large apartment in Trump Tower. Trump's office is also in Trump Tower. She said being close to work makes her life easier. Trump can get home in a few minutes. This allows her to spend more time with her children.

THE OLD POST OFFICE

The Old Post Office was built in 1899. It was the post office of Washington, DC, and the US Post Office headquarters. The Old Post Office takes up an entire city block. In 2014, the Trump Organization got permission to renovate the building. Trump called the renovation one of her career highlights. She visited the site at least once a week. She made sure the historic building was carefully restored.

Throughout 2016, Trump helped her father campaign for the presidency. She appeared many times to support Donald and speak on his behalf. Her speech at the Republican National Convention was one of many ways she supported him.

Ivanka Trump campaigned for her father in the 2016 presidential election.

PRESIDENTIAL DAUGHTER

Trump stood by her father in the early hours of November 9, 2016. Donald Trump had just won the presidential election. After a short night's sleep, Trump was seen on the streets in New York City. It was back to business for Trump. She was now the daughter of the 45th president, but there was still work to be done.

STRAIGHT TO THE SOURCE

When *Business Insider* asked how she makes the right hiring choices, Trump replied:

> *We want self-starters. We want people who are optimistic, who see challenges as opportunities. People who are dedicated, who really are accountable to one another and toward achieving shared goals, who are ambitious. I like people who aren't shy about the use of that word.*
>
> *It's always a huge red flag for me when somebody's . . . a little slow in providing thoughtful references that are a testament to them as a person and their professional accomplishments. I'm also really surprised how few people call for references. That's almost the most basic thing one can do to assess them.*

Source: Rachel Gillett. "Ivanka Trump Shares the One Thing She Always Does before Offering Someone a Job." *Business Insider*. Business Insider, March 18, 2016. Web. February 9, 2017.

What's the Big Idea?

In a paragraph, explain what Trump believes makes a good worker. Use details from the text to support your argument. Do you agree with Trump about what makes a person a good worker?

IMPORTANT DATES

1981
Ivanka Trump is born in New York City on October 30.

1992
Trump's parents divorce.

1999
Trump enrolls at Georgetown University.

2002
Trump transfers to the Wharton School.

2004
Trump graduates from the Wharton School; she begins work at Forest City Ratner.

2005
Trump becomes vice president of development and acquisitions at the Trump Organization.

2006
Trump begins appearing on *The Apprentice*.

2007
Trump founds Trump Hotels with her brothers and starts Ivanka Trump Fine Jewelry.

2009
Trump marries Jared Kushner, converts to Judaism, and publishes *The Trump Card: Playing to Win in Work and Life.*

2015
Trump introduces her father when he announces he is running for president on June 16.

2016
Trump introduces her father at the Republican National Convention on July 21.

2017
Nordstrom stops selling products from the Ivanka Trump Collection.

STOP AND THINK

Surprise Me

Chapter Two discussed the jobs Trump and her brothers had as teenagers. Later, Trump worked as a model to earn money of her own. Did you find this surprising? Write a paragraph telling why or why not.

Why Do I Care?

Maybe you have never encountered Trump's business projects. But that doesn't mean you can't think about the ways Trump has targeted working women. Do you think she is a good role model for young women who want to work in the business world? Why or why not? Write a paragraph explaining your thoughts.

You Are There

Trump introduced her father at the 2016 Republican National Convention. Imagine you are asked to give a speech introducing a family member at a major event. What kind of things would you say?

Say What?

Reading about business can mean learning some new words. Find five words in this book that you have never heard before. Look in a dictionary to find their meanings. Write the meanings in your own words and use each word in a new sentence.

GLOSSARY

campaign
activities done to get voters to elect a person to a political office

construction
the building of a large structure

delegates
people who are chosen to speak or act for others

elite
the best of something that is sometimes not available to everyone

empire
a group of companies that are controlled by one person

nominate
the act of choosing a person to run for office

real estate
property of buildings or land

recession
a temporary period of reduced economic activity in a country

renovate
to repair or rebuild parts of an existing building

LEARN MORE

Books

Bjornlund, Lydia. *Modern Political Parties.* Minneapolis, MN: Abdo Publishing, 2016.

Davies, Jacqueline. *The Lemonade War*. Boston: Houghton Mifflin, 2007.

Kopp, Megan. *Reality Television*. Minneapolis, MN: Abdo Publishing, 2013.

Websites

To learn more about Newsmakers, visit **abdobooklinks.com**. These links are routinely monitored and updated to provide the most current information available.

Visit **abdocorelibrary.com** for free additional tools for teachers and students.

INDEX

About the Author

Bonnie Hinman has written more than 40 nonfiction books for kids. She likes to learn about all the interesting people in the news. Hinman lives in Southwest Missouri with her husband, Bill, and near her children and five grandchildren.